IMAGES OF IRELAND

SOUTH DUBLIN

FROM THE LIFFEY TO GREYSTONES

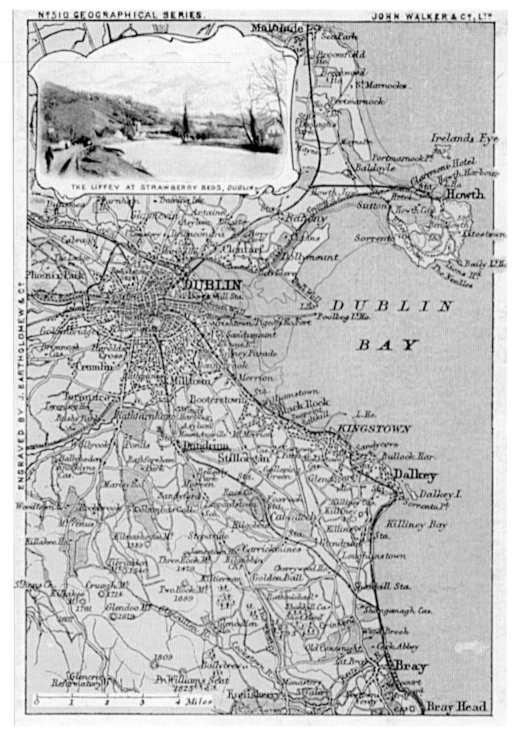

THE LIFFEY AT STRAWBERRY BEDS, DUBLIN.

ENGRAVED BY J. BARTHOLOMEW & Cº

A postcard by John Walker & Co. Ltd showing South Dublin and Dublin Bay, c.1903.

IMAGES OF IRELAND

SOUTH DUBLIN

FROM THE LIFFEY TO GREYSTONES

DEREK STANLEY

NONSUCH

The Kingstown coat of arms. Around 1760, there was a small harbour at Dunleary which after some years filled with sand and became useless. In 1817, work commenced on building a new harbour and the East Pier. In 1821, when the East Pier was almost finished, King George IV departed from Dunleary after a state visit to Dublin. In his honour, the town was renamed 'Kingstown'. Within five years of the new harbour being built, the town had become the principal mail and passenger port linking Britain and Ireland. Transport links to Dublin were further improved with the opening of the Dublin to Kingstown railway line in 1834. The name of the town reverted to Dun Laoghaire in 1920.

First published by Gill & Macmillan 2000
This edition published by Nonsuch 2006

Nonsuch Publishing
73 Lower Leeson Street
Dublin 2
Ireland
www.nonsuchireland.com

British Library Cataloguing in Publication Data.
A catalogue record for this book is available from the British Library.

ISBN 1 84588 566 X
ISBN-13 1 84588 566 3

Typesetting and origination by Tempus Publishing Limited
Printed in Great Britain

Contents

Acknowledgements

I am grateful to my friends and family, who have helped me by providing photographs, inspiration and information for this book. In particular, I should like to thank Kitty Brooks, Barbara McCarthy, Pat O'Brien, Fergal MacAlister, Joan O'Byrne, Peter O'Hara, George Corbett, Martin Gordon and my wife Theresa, who has provided me with so much support and encouragement.

A view by the artist Walter Hayward Young (Jotter), c.1910, showing the Coningbeg and Skulmartin Lightships in Kingstown Harbour. Along the East Coast, from Belfast Lough to Cork Harbour, the great reefs and sandbanks had nine light vessels to mark the hazards for all sailors. These were Skulmartin and South Rock off the Down Coast, Kish at the entrance to Dublin Bay, Codling off the Wicklow coast, Arklow and Blackwater off the North Wexford coast, Barrels and Coningbeg off the South Wexford coast and Daunts at the entrance to Cork Harbour. The two vessels shown would have been visiting the maintenance depot of the Commissioner for Irish Lights, which was established at Kingstown Harbour in 1875.

Introduction

South Dublin and the coastal suburbs are an area of great natural beauty. The city has now expanded, but previously there were leafy suburbs with rows of distinguished houses and small picturesque villages surrounded by attractive countryside. The scenic coastline has cliffs, sandy beaches, fine harbours and seaside resorts with splendid promenades. The region lies in the shelter of the Wicklow mountains.

It is difficult to do the area justice in a book of this size. The photographs and postcards have been chosen to give a 'flavour' of South Dublin and its history. The problem has been what to leave out rather than what to include. The dates are often based on postmarks on the cards, which is normally a good guide. However, it is possible that images may have been photographed several years earlier. Some of the postcard images may not have the clarity of Fr Browne's photographs, or the rarity of those in the O'Connor collection, but they do provide a fascinating record of people, places and buildings within the past hundred years. Much has changed in that time and many of the views show streets and buildings, which are now completely altered, or sometimes have been demolished.

This book gives a brief glimpse of the coastal suburbs and area south of Dublin. With each image there is some narrative, but this is not in any way a complete text. Hopefully, readers will find the images and script both interesting and enjoyable. Everybody is likely to have an area of special interest and it would be a bonus if they were inspired to do further research into the history of particular photographs. For some people the photographs will evoke nostalgic memories of the past. This is valuable, as often at the time of an event there is little appreciation of the true significance of what is taking place. In fact, opinions are often expressed after a building has gone and, unfortunately, by then the situation is irreversible. Today there is more commitment to preserving our heritage. In South Dublin there are many fine buildings and places which benefit from preservation and protection.

There have been many social and physical changes in South Dublin in the past century. This publication is a limited pictorial record charting local buildings and events, which shows some of those changes. For older people it will jog memories and for the younger age group it will provide some insight into their local history. I hope that everybody who reads the book will find it a happy and rewarding experience.

Derek Stanley, 2000.

Kingstown Harbour, *c*.1890. There are two paddle ships lying alongside the Carlisle Pier and one anchored in the harbour. After 1884, the City of Dublin Company ran four steamers between Kingstown and Holyhead which were the *Ulster, Munster, Leinster* and *Connaught*. A fifth ship, the *Ireland*, was added to the fleet in 1885. The constant hard service of these vessels is shown by the paint-blistered funnels of the ship on the right, which is berthed at the Pier. The three imposing buildings on the skyline are from left to right, the Royal Marine Hotel, the original St Michael's church with its square tower, and the Town Hall. The Pavilion has yet to be built.

One

Irishtown, Sandymount, Ballsbridge and Donnybrook

The Allen A. Ryan Home Hospital, Pigeon House Road, South Wall of the Liffey, c.1917. Patients are shown working in the vegetable gardens with Dublin Bay in the background. The hospital, which had thirty-five beds and treated patients with cholera, was located away from the city centre to try to isolate it from areas of fever and infection. In the 1930s, the hospital became a TB sanatorium under the care of the French Sisters of St Vincent de Paul.

Crowds on the South Wall watch the Isle of Man boat departing from the mouth of the Liffey. In the seventeenth century, ships with deep hulls had to anchor off Ringsend, which was also the base for the Dublin fishing industry. However, the river Dodder cut Ringsend off from Dublin so the Ballast Committee for Dublin Port decided to build a North and South Wall for the Liffey. This involved widening and deepening the river and diverting the course of the Dodder. The South Wall with the Poolbeg Lighthouse was completed by 1796. Ringsend, at the Pigeonhouse Harbour (named after Mr Pidgeon, who sold refreshments to passengers from his home), was the main landing place for the Liverpool packet boats until their transfer to Howth Harbour around 1800.

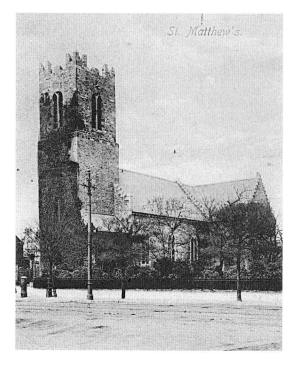

St Matthew's church, Irishtown, c.1905. The church was built on this site for Dublin Corporation in 1706, to be used by mariners and fishermen. The square tower, designed by Richard Mills, was added in 1713. The area was a haunt for smugglers, who are said to have regularly hidden prohibited goods in the tower. In 1878, the church was completely rebuilt. In 1905, Irishtown was a maritime village, in the parish of St Mary's, Donnybrook, with two streets and a fine strand. It was a few hundred yards from Ringsend and was a popular place for sea bathing.

Strand Road, Sandymount, *c.*1930. A peaceful scene as riders exercise their horses on the long sandy beach. In James Joyce's *Ulysses*, Stephen Daedalus walked along the beach 'into eternity along Sandymount Strand'. The rectangular structure, just seen to the left of the Martello Tower, is an open sea swimming bath (see pp. 26 and 27).

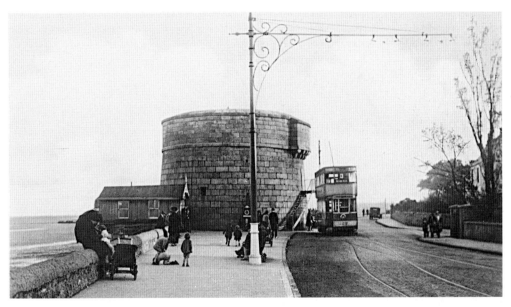

The Martello Tower at Sandymount, *c.*1930. The name came from a tower in Cape Martello in Corsica, which had been captured by the British in 1793. Twenty-one of these circular towers costing £1,800 each, with granite walls which were nine feet thick, were built on the coast between 1804 and 1806. Each one held a small garrison and they were meant to give early warning and also oppose any possible landing of Napoleon's troops. The tower at Sandymount was built on the sandbank and did not have rock foundations. It had to be supported on large oaken beams. It had no proper road until Strand Road was built in the 1830s.

Star of the Sea church, Sandymount, was designed by J. J. McCarthy and opened in 1853. A new parish was created out of a part of Donnybrook and Irishtown. It was an attractive church with three almost equal gables, which then stood very near the seashore. James Joyce features the church in the Nausicaa section of *Ulysses*, when Leopold Bloom comes to Sandymount Strand. He had previously written from Trieste in 1920 to his Aunt Josephine, who lived off the North Strand Road, enquiring if there were trees (and of what kind) behind the church visible from the shore and if there were steps leading down at the side of the church from Leahy's Terrace. The building of a sea wall, houses and a new road in the 1920s distanced the church from the seashore.

Sandymount Green, c.1910. In the eighteenth century, a village called 'Brickfield Town' stood here, for workers from Lord Merrion's brickfields. The clay in the area made good bricks and they were used to build many Georgian Dublin houses. However, the village changed its name and because of its fine sandy beach, excellent bathing and proximity to Dublin, Sandymount became a popular seaside resort. Sunday outings to pick cockles were a favourite pastime for Dubliners. However, the beach was fairly exclusive and bathers were charged twopence, whereas at Irishtown the charge was just one penny. By the early nineteenth century, the Green was the hub of the village, having a hotel and several lodging houses. Highwaymen were particularly active in the area, so visitors would stay overnight rather than risk the journey to town in the dark.

Haddington Road, *c.*1910. This is a fashionable road in a wooded area formerly known as 'Beggar's Bush', where beggars used to shelter before heading for the city. At the end of the terrace on the right is the tower of St Mary's church. The church was built in 1839 and the tower added in 1894. In the early 1900s, St Mary's was one of the wealthiest parishes in Dublin. It was the only Catholic church in Dublin to erect a memorial plaque to honour those parishioners who fought and died in the First World War.

Adelaide Road, *c.*1919. This was named after Queen Adelaide, the wife of William IV. The road had a number of important buildings including the Royal Victoria Eye and Ear Hospital, a Jewish synagogue, a Catholic Apostolic church and a Presbyterian church. In 1919, the road surface was much worse than today. However, the main central Dublin streets would have been tarred. The bridge over the road in the distance carries the railway line from Harcourt Street station towards Bray.

Mr J. Byrne's horse, Jim, and a cart from the Pembroke Dairy carrying a milk churn. They look very smart and were the winners of the first prize in the Royal Dublin Society Shows at Ballsbridge in 1909 and 1910.

R.J. Mecredy, Hon. secretary of the Automobile Club of Ireland, known as 'RJ', at the wheel of an early motor vehicle, c. 1903. The driver was an Irish cycling champion, who became a pioneer of motoring in Ireland. As editor of the *Motor News*, which he founded in 1900, he did much to popularize the hobby.

Upper Baggot Street, *c.*1905. The tram in the centre, having crossed Baggot Street Bridge over the Grand Canal and passed the Royal City of Dublin Hospital, is outside a grand row of shops including Findlaters and William Davy, both grocers and wine merchants. The shops gave an old-style personal service and catered for the community living in the large houses in the area, which included Waterloo, Wellington and Pembroke Roads.

Ballsbridge Road, *c.*1906. A quiet scene as tram no. 284 heads for Nelson's Pillar. The railings on the right surround Herbert Park, which was the site for the 1907 International Exhibition. On the left, there is a drinking trough for horses.

Stillorgan Road, Donnybrook, c. 1910. It is not surprising that the trams were the most popular form of transport as, in 1910, there were services to and from Dublin every ten minutes! On the left, is the Sacred Heart church in Donnybrook, which was designed by Pugin and Ashlin. It was built of granite with Bath stone dressings and cost £6,000. The church was dedicated by Dr Paul Cullen, the Cardinal Archbishop, on 26 August 1866. As Donnybrook increased in population, the church was extended in 1928.

The Sacred Heart Parish, Donnybrook, Boys' Club under fifteens' soccer team, 1965/66. From left to right, back row: V. O'Connor, P. Kelly, A. Carroll, B. Fox, T. Wright, T. Gorman, P. Kearns, C. Lester. Front row: T. Daly, D. Breen, N. Hanky, C. Doyle, P. Wright.

Two

Rathmines, Rathgar and Terenure

RATHMINES ROAD, RATHMINES.

Lower Rathmines Road from Portobello, *c.*1930. On the left of the road is a fine terrace including the church of Our Lady of Refuge. At the end of the road is the clock tower of Rathmines Town Hall. A horse-drawn water wagon heads in the direction of the Town Hall.

A busy scene in Rathmines, *c.*1924, looking north from Upper Rathmines Road. On the right is Alex Findlater & Co. Ltd, wine merchants and grocers, with their distinctive clock, made by Chancellor and Sons of Dublin. Findlater's was a well-known business which had a large store in O'Connell Street and branches throughout the city and suburbs.

Rathmines Town Hall, *c.*1920. This fine red sandstone building was designed by Sir Thomas Drew and built in 1887. The clock was made by Chancellor and Sons of Dublin in 1894. The building was the focal point for town business and also a venue for concerts, dances and meetings. Marconi demonstrated his wireless telegraph from the clock tower in 1896 and one of Edison's first 'moving films' was shown in the hall in 1902. Percy French performed there regularly and speakers at meetings included William Butler Yeats, Liam O'Flaherty and Douglas Hyde.

The 21st Dublin Company Boys' Brigade soccer team, 1905/06. From left to right, back row: S. Tomlin, C. Blythe, W. Graham, C. Keely, L. Jewell (honorary secretary). Middle row: J. MacDonagh, A. Hall, H. Tomlin (Capt.), R. Gibson, S. Young. Front row: W. Young, A. Black. The card, postmarked July 1907, states that these are some of our 'Rathmines Boys'. However, the Boys' Brigade was also well known for its band, which regularly marched through Rathmines.

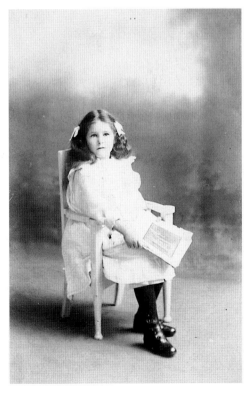

A pretty young girl poses for the photographer at Mr James E. Behan's studio at 150 Rathmines Road, c.1910.

St Mary's College, Rathmines, rugby football team for the 1973/74 season. They were winners of the Leinster Junior Cup with a 10-4 victory over Belvedere in the final. From left to right, back row: P. Barnwell, F. McEntee, P. Davitt, T. Kennedy, B. Quigley, M. Fitzgerald, P. Gueret. front row: D. Cowman, K. Holland, W. Opperman, K. Egan (captain), R. McDonnell, T. Coveney, G. Coman. St Mary's first Junior Cup victory was in 1934 and they won their first Leinster Senior Cup in 1961.

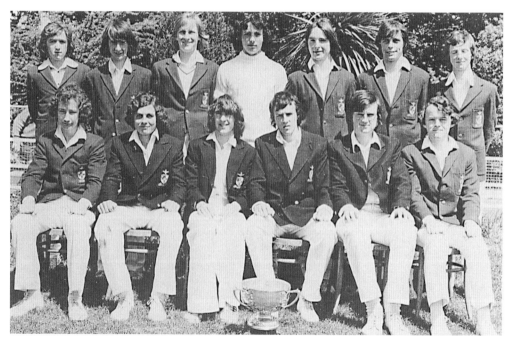

St Mary's College senior cricket XI in 1974, winners of the Leinster Senior Cricket Cup. From left to right, back row: C. O'Neill, D. Lonergan, B. Foley, P. Healy, R. McDonnell, B. Quigley, P. Walsh. front row: K. Egan, R. Sloan, D. McCarthy, N. Smith (captain), G. McDonald, B. Quigley.

Rathgar, *c.*1910. The village is situated midway between Rathmines and Terenure and the tram heads towards Terenure. The church at the junction of Rathgar Road and Highfield Road is Christchurch, which was designed by the Scottish architect, Andrew Heiton, and opened in 1859. On the left, the shop at 107 Rathgar Road, with the empty cart outside, is J. & R. Hanlon, victuallers.

The Rathgar saw mills, *c.*1918. The factory, owned by Locke and Woods, was sited on the banks of the River Dodder above the weir. The tall chimney was a local landmark.

Terenure, c.1950. The first horse tram ran from College Green to Terenure on 1 February 1872. Some eighty years later there had been a great improvement in speed and design. Tram car no. 131, outside McIntyre's newsagents, has a domed roof and passengers travel in comfort. The building on the right is the Dublin United Tramways Office.

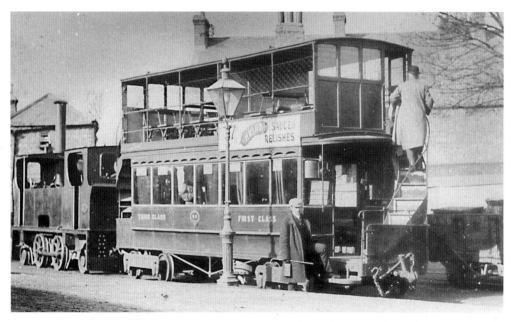

Passengers mount the 'Scrap-Iron Express', c.1910. The Dublin and Blessington Steam Tramway opened in 1888. The city trams would terminate at Terenure. Passengers would change to the Steam Tramway, which ran to Blessington at the foot of the Dublin Mountains. It was a popular excursion for tourists and day trippers. At one time there were plans to take the line over the Wicklow Gap to Glendalough, but the proposed extension never took place. In 1929, buses began running direct from the city to Wicklow. After this the numbers using the Steam Tramway declined. It was eventually closed down in 1932.

Carmelite College, Terenure, Dublin.

The Carmelite College, Upper Terenure Road. The house was purchased from the Bourne family in 1860 by the Carmelites, who opened it as a secondary school. The friars are walking by the lake, which is fed by a tributary of the Swan river.

Happy faces in the Terenure College junior under-twelves' rugby team, 1943.

Terenure College Old Boys' rugby football team in 1953/54, the season they won the Leinster Junior League Cup.

Terenure College Old Boys' rugby football team, *c.*1965/66. There are many new faces, but some of the victorious cup squad from 1953/54 are still playing. In the centre of the back row wearing the white scrum cap is Stan Brooks.

Three

Milltown, Merrion, Booterstown and Blackrock

Milltown, *c.*1911: a peaceful, pretty village with family-run shops. It was a favourite residential suburb and, being only three miles from Dublin, visitors would travel out by coach for rural recreation and fresh air in Milltown Park.

A peaceful scene as people stroll on the banks of the River Dodder near Milltown, *c.*1930.

The Merrion Pier and Swimming Baths located just beyond the Sandymount Martello Tower, *c.*1905. They were designed by Frederick Morley and opened in 1882. The original plans included a pier extending for three miles out to sea, but this idea was impractical. In fact, when it was completed, the pier had an iron structure with a timber deck and ran for 300 yards from the sea wall. There were kiosks at the entrance on the Strand Road and, along the pier, there were wicker tables and chairs. A band would play in the large shelter halfway along its length on each Tuesday and Saturday during the summer months and on most Sunday afternoons. The swimming baths were filled with fresh seawater and measured 120 by 120ft, equally divided for ladies and gentlemen.

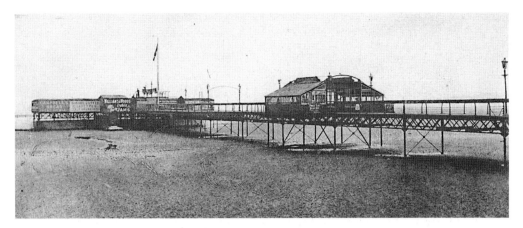

Merrion Promenade Pier and Swimming Baths, c.1908. At the end of the pier on the landward side of the baths were the changing-rooms and some sideshows. The card shows hoardings advertising Campbell's Bread, Donore Castle Cigarettes and Williams & Wood's Dublin Jams. The Baths Company did very well for some years, but attendances declined and the project went out of business in the early 1920s. The iron pier was sold as scrap to Hammond Lane Foundry.

The Blind Institute, Merrion, c.1910. Merrion Castle was built on this site by Thomas Bagod of the Baggotrath family in 1334. It was acquired by the Fitzwilliams in the early fifteenth century. Nearby was the area of clay which Lord Merrion used for making bricks in the eighteenth century. The Irish Sisters of Charity bought the land and remnants of the old castle in 1866, building a convent and founding St Mary's Home for the Blind. In 1912, there were 182 female residents in the home, who were supported, clothed and trained for work. In 1921, during the Civil War, some British soldiers in an open tender accompanied by an armoured car, travelling from Kingstown to Dublin Castle, were ambushed by a small group of Volunteers from behind the wall of the convent. Two soldiers were killed, but the armoured car could not break down the gates and the ambush party got safely away.

A peaceful scene in Booterstown, c.1910. Booterstown was then a suburban village within easy reach of Dublin, where many professional people lived. The grocer and wine merchant, J.P. & E. McCabe, is on the corner. Booterstown once had a sandy beach, but the building of the Dublin-Kingstown Railway made a marsh area, which is now a bird sanctuary.

St Philip's and St James's church, Booterstown, c.1908. The church was designed by John Bowden with a square tower, battlements and a tall spire. It cost £5,000 and opened in May, 1824. There have been many distinguished parishioners including the D'Olier family, who lived in Booterstown Avenue. When Eamon De Valera opened the National School in the church grounds in 1957, he said that, as a Booterstown resident, he had heard the church bells ringing for almost sixty years and they had always brought him peace, calm, quiet and contentment.

Mount Merrion Avenue, *c*.1920. On the right is St Andrew's Presbyterian church, opened in 1899. In the 1890s, John Boyd Dunlop, the inventor of the pneumatic tyre, lived at Talbot House (no. 95). At the end of the avenue, beside Rock Road, overlooking the park and Dublin Bay, is the house 'Líon an Uisce'(or Lisnaskea). In the eighteenth century, Lady Arabella Denny lived there for forty-four years. She was the first woman member of the Royal Dublin Society and is said to have introduced carpet weaving to Ireland. She also tried to breed silkworms at the house. John Wesley was very complimentary about the house when he visited in 1783, saying, 'it was one of the pleasantest spots I ever saw.'

Blackrock Park, *c*.1910. After the Dublin to Kingstown Railway was built in 1834, the area between the track and Rock Road became very marshy. After some years, under the Towns Improvement Act, this swampland was developed into a formal Victorian park, which was laid out in the 1870s and incorporated the 'Vauxhall Gardens'. The park covered fourteen acres, including two ornamental lakes.

Idrone Terrace from the Railway Bridge, Blackrock, overlooking Dublin Bay, *c*.1920. This formal terrace of twenty-seven houses was built around 1850 on land owned by Dr Henry Kavanagh, an apothecary in Kingstown. The central block on the terrace has a plaque which carries the grand name 'Idrone sur Mer'. The houses were large, but they needed no stables, as they were so near the railway.

Idrone Terrace, Blackrock, *c*.1925. The writer of the card, on 22 June, 1925, says he is staying at his sister's house (marked X), for the wedding of her daughter. He comments on the wonderful sea view from the house.

Main Street, Blackrock, *c.*1907. On the right, there is a crowd of children, posing for the photographer. They stand outside Alex Findlater & Co., grocers and wine merchants, with its distinctive clock. On the left, directly opposite, is the Ulster Bank, which was designed by W.M. Mitchell and built in 1892.

Main Street, Blackrock, *c.*1907. The crowd is standing in front of James Quinn, grocer, wine and spirit merchant. The photographer is the centre of attention.

The entrance to Linden Convalescent Home, Blackrock, *c.*1950. The home was founded in 1864 by the Sisters of Charity, who ran St Vincent's Hospital in Stephens Green, to cater for the poor. Male and female patients were admitted free from fourteen Dublin city hospitals. It was an ideal place for recuperation, with its beautiful tree-lined grounds in which the patients could walk or rest in the shade. In 1912, there was accommodation for sixty-three patients and around 1,200 patients were treated each year. Father Frank Browne (1880-1960), who took photographs on the *Titanic* and also took many outstanding pictures of Dublin, was a patient here in 1939,

Boys play cricket at Linden, *c.*1950. The wicket appears to have tumbled.

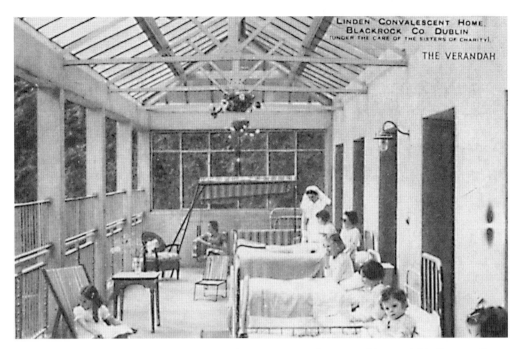

The children's beds on the veranda at Linden, *c.*1950. 'Fresh air, sunshine and Bird's custard' was the prescription for convalescence.

Sports day at the Military Hospital in Blackrock on 8 May 1918. It was a convalescent hospital and regular sports and games helped the soldiers to recover more quickly from their injuries. For this race, the competitors are on their marks and lined up for a sprint. The starter stands behind them. It is probable that some soldiers have had eye injuries in the war, as they are wearing blindfolds. The sacks for the sack race lie ready in the foreground.

The Town Hall and Carnegie Library, Blackrock, c.1912. They are ornate buildings. The Town Hall was completed in 1866 and the Library in 1889. The entrance to the fire station is in the foreground.

Carysfort Avenue, Blackrock, c.1910. A peaceful suburban road with the Protestant church on the left. In 1892, James Joyce, at the age of ten, lived at a house called Leoville (no. 23) for just over a year. He often visited Blackrock Park or would go bathing at the foot of the Martello Tower at Seapoint.

Williamstown Castle, Blackrock College, *c.* 1910. This house and grounds were purchased by the Holy Ghost Fathers in 1875. It became part of Blackrock College, which had been founded in 1860, at Castle Dawson House. Williamstown Castle was rebuilt and extended in 1905-06, to a design by the Revd Fr J.M. Ebenrecht, who added large three-storey wings with corner towers and battlements in the style of the original castle. The college continued to expand and, in 1924, Willow Park was purchased. This became a preparatory school for the college in 1935.

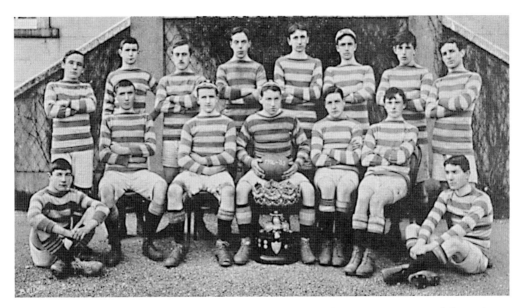

Blackrock College rugby football team in 1904/05, when they were winners of the Leinster Schools Challenge Cup. From left to right, back row: T. Sheehan, T.J. Bligh, J.P. Roche, H. Harbison, J.M. Talty, J. Seymour, T. Collins, P. Kelly. front row: Joseph Quinn, M. Rohan, A.J. O'Connor, W.J. Sweeney (captain), J. Lawlor, J. Healy, J. Metcalfe.

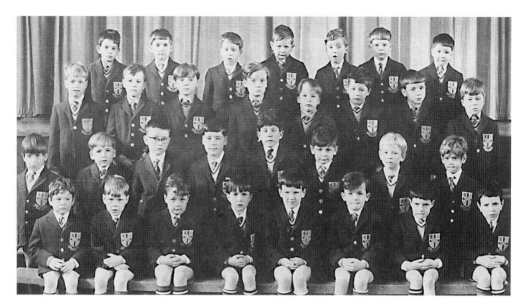

St Michael's School kindergarten, Blackrock College, 1968/69. From left to right, back row: P. Dixon, E. Scaife, S. Kilcoyne, J. Crowley, M. Sheehan, W. Atkinson, F. Rhatigan. Third row: J. Muldowney, M. Young, D. Gleeson, E. O'Mahoney, F. Hughes, J. Hughes, J. Molony, A. Campbell. second row: P. Quinn, G. Hannon, C. Lyons, A. McCarthy, R. Stanton, W. O'Brien, P. Broy, A. Smurfit. front row: M. Simpson, R. Cuddy, N. Meehan, P. Gately, B. Quirk, M. Duff, N. McAuley, C. Mount.

The Willow Park School Band, Blackrock College, 1978. From left to right, back row: F. Murray, C. Murphy, R. Cullen, P. Mahon. Second row: W. O'Leary, B. Cronin, N. O'Brolchain, D. Kelly, M. Ward, J. Forrest, F. Cronin, D. O'Keefe, T. Crotty, D. Horgan. front row: P. Ryan, N. White, E. Daly, C. Lenihan, Fr J. Dowling, C. Gregg, E. Kenny, P. Kearney, B. Walsh.

Blackrock College rugby football team, winners of the Leinster Schools Challenge Cup in the 1914/15 season. During the season, the team played thirteen matches, winning twelve and losing one. They scored a total of 205 points and had only 25 points scored against them. From left to right, back row: J. Meehan, S. Wallis, M. Walshe, P. Kelly, P. O'Sullivan, S. McCormick. Middle row: J. Cleary, V. Coghlan, J. Walshe, J. Gordon (captain), M. Mullins, J. Malone, L. Wallace. Front row: S. O'Carroll, W. Prior.

Blackrock College Junior Rugby Cup team, winners of the Leinster Schools' Cup, 1968/69. From left to right, back row: M. O'Sullivan, J. Rekab, P. McGuinness, J. McManus, B. McCormack, B. Curtin, G. McConnell. Middle row: D. G. O'Reilly, A. Moran, C. Doris, J. Cantrell (captain), P. Forte, S. Hall, F. Connolly. Front row: F. Canavan, R. Caulfield.

Blackrock College senior Gaelic football team, 1979/80. From left to right, back row: M. Walshe, D. McCaffrey, M. Aylmer, N. O'Sullivan, R. Kevany, K. Sweeney, A. Lynch, S. Murphy, D. McCarthy, J. O'Boyle. Middle row: J. Barry, J. Garvey, J. Hurley, D. Sweeney (captain), J. McMahon, J. Delaney, P. Coghlan. Front row: D. Murnane, A. Berwick, P. Mahony, W. Walshe.

Blackrock College Swimming Club, 1979/80. From left to right, back row: M. Davis, C. O'Donoghue, B. Kehoe, L. Shanahan, D. McCarthy, A. Harbison (captain), G. Cronin, M. Hyland, B. Kenny, J. Rafter. Middle row: R. Cullen, J. Rogers, J. Rafter, D. Connolly, M. Mansfield, B. Cronin. Front row: P. Kehoe, P. O'Neill, S. Dufficy, F. O'Beirne, D. Heavey.

St Catherine's Convent, Sion Hill, Blackrock, c.1935. The house was built in 1792 on a hill near the Three Rock Mountain in about 9 acres of land overlooking the sea, where there were rare shrubs growing, brought from the Holy Land. In 1840, the Dominican Sisters, who had a small school at 88 Lower Mount Street, moved here and opened the convent. Over the next fifty years, as pupil numbers increased, much development took place. The view shows the three-storey convent building, with its central block and wings with arched recesses containing windows and statues on each side. The convent had famous visitors including Father Matthew in 1842 and Daniel O'Connell in 1846. The school was very progressive and had a high academic and musical reputation. Sport was encouraged and in 1900, the girls played tennis, croquet and, surprisingly, cricket. In the summer, they went swimming at Blackrock Baths.

St Catherine's Higher School of Domestic Economy, Sion Hill Dominican Convent, c.1915. A training school for domestic science teachers was started in 1910, but it was not until 1929 that St Catherine's was recognized by the Department of Education. The convent at Sion Hill celebrated its centenary in 1936. At that time, the senior school had 186 boarders and day pupils.

Left: Harpists at Sion Hill Convent in 1977. Back row: Sheila Glynn, Tanya Glynn, Julie Walters, Hilary Maxwell. Front row: Daphne Quigley, –?–. Sion Hill Convent has a fine musical tradition and past pupils, who became well-known harpists, include Mary O'Hara, Deirdre Flynn, Kathleen Watkins and Deirdre O'Callaghan.

Below: A happy group of students at Sion Hill Convent in Summer 1977. From left to right: Hilary Maxwell, Niamh Walsh, Margaret Grace, Ibifuro Fiberessma and Rita Murphy. The tower and steeple of St Phillip's and St James's church, Blackrock is in the background.

Four

Goatstown, Dundrum, Stillorgan and Monkstown

Goatstown, Dundrum, Co. Dublin, *c.*1907. Children gather outside the village shop of A.E. Traynor, family grocer. The area was known for its goat herds and dairy farms.

The Main Street, Dundrum, *c.*1907. A peaceful scene as a lone cyclist travels down the middle of the street. The village, situated at the base of the Dublin Mountains, on the road to Enniskerry, was a popular health resort, known for the purity of its air. Invalids, who visited the village in September each year, would drink the local goat's milk, which was thought to be a cure for consumption (otherwise known as TB).

The Manor Hill Laundry, Dundrum, *c.*1905. The laundry was established in 1876 in the valley below Dundrum castle, where the stream once powered the Manor corn mill. It soon expanded and became a large employer in the surrounding area. The card shows the extensive buildings. At the left hand corner, laundry is shown hanging out to dry. In the factory some washing was done by hand. The washerwomen had to work in their bare feet as much water splashed on to the floor. The laundry closed in the 1940s.

Convent of the Sacred Heart, Mount Anville, Dundrum, *c.*1905. The house was built around 1800, but was much improved by William Dargan, the railway engineer, who lived there from 1840 to 1866 and added the tower and gate-lodge. He organized the Great Exhibition in Dublin in 1853. Queen Victoria visited the Great Exhibition and also came to Mount Anville. In 1912, the convent was a boarding school for young ladies and the Revd Mother Superior was a 'Madame Thunder'! The nuns also taught at the Convent National Schools, which had 140 pupils.

The Peach House, Convent of the Sacred Heart, Mount Anville, Dundrum, *c.*1910. There were greenhouses and vineyards at the convent and the good summers would produce bumper crops of fruit.

Grove View, Stillorgan, County Dublin, *c*.1915. There is an advertisement on the wall of Grove View House for J. & J. Cullen, grocer and publican. James Byrne's dairy is on the right. The village had no tram service but from 1854 it was served by the Harcourt Street railway line. The railway station was in Brewery Road, near the Stillorgan Reservoir, about a mile from the village. However, in 1910, there was an excellent train service. Each weekday there were sixteen trains to the city, the journey taking seventeen minutes, and every Sunday there were fourteen trains to Bray. Unfortunately, the line was closed in 1958.

Vartry Reservoir, Stillorgan, *c*.1918. This large reservoir to serve the City of Dublin was built by Dublin Corporation in 1884. The edge of the grey stone pump-house, which has an octagonal design, is shown on the left.

Above: Patients walk beside the Napier Wing of the Convalescent Home at Brewery Road, Stillorgan, *c.*1913. The home was built in 1865 and has a gabled front and a small rooftop cupola. The locality was renowned for the freshness of its air, which was considered favourable to health.

Right: Ladies playing croquet in the grounds of St Kevin's Holiday Home, Kilmacud Road, Stillorgan, *c.*1908. The house, Redesdale, was built around 1790. It became a retreat house in 1903 and was called St Kevin's Park. In 1910, it became the 'Irish Training School of Domestic Economy', run by the Department of Agriculture and Technical Instruction.

The Crescent, Monkstown, c.1910. In the centre, facing the Dublin Road is the distinctive Monkstown Church of Ireland church, with its 'Moorish' appearance. It was designed by John Semple in 1833. The new church, which replaced a small rectangular building, had seating for 800 people. It was built with corner towers, battlements and a large central tower. Not all of the comments at the time were favourable and some critics said the pinnacles looked like pawns in a chess game. It became known as the 'chessmen church'. On the right of the picture, situated on Carrickbrennan Road, is St Patrick's Catholic church, which was designed in the French Gothic style by Pugin and Ashlin and completed in 1866.

Alma Nurseries, 53 Monkstown Road, c.1920. The nurseries were managed by William McClatchie and Sons. A gardener is shown working in one of the tomato houses. Further down the road, the Montpelier Nursery was at no. 29. At that time, the Monkstown area had several nurseries, as flowers and plants thrived in the mild climate.

A train steams into Salthill station, Monkstown, *c.*1930. Schoolboys are waiting on the platform. The railway ran from Westland Row in Dublin to Kingstown. It was officially opened to the public on 17 December 1834. The station had a superb position on the bay and was described as looking like a 'Swiss chalet'. A distinguishing feature was the tall chimneys, which can be seen on the photograph. The advertising hoardings include posters for Switzer's Summer Sale and for the Kingstown Regatta.

The Salthill Hotel, Monkstown, *c.*1915. There were salt works here during the eighteenth century and a large house called Salthill, which looked over Dunleary Harbour. The house was purchased by the Railway Company and using plans drawn up by John Skipton Mulvaney was incorporated into the Salthill Hotel. Thackeray wrote favourably of the hotel in his *Irish Sketch Book* of 1844. The business did very well and, in 1865, the hotel was improved and enlarged in a 'French Chateau' style, by the architect, John McCurdy, who had also designed the Royal Marine Hotel in Kingstown. Unfortunately, the hotel was destroyed by fire in 1973.

CBC Monkstown rugby football squad, 1982 – All Ireland Schools Sevens winners. The team was coached by Mick Mullen.

Seapoint, c.1950. A popular bathing place for many years. Seapoint baths, described as the 'ladies' bathing place', was built by the railway company around 1840. The Martello Tower was built in 1805 and could only be reached by crossing the Ordnance Bridge.

Five

Dun Laoghaire/ Kingstown

A view of Kingstown Harbour by the artist Walter Hayward Young, known as 'Jotter' (see p. 6), around 1910. Crowds of visitors stroll along the East Pier, walking as far as the lighthouse and viewing the activity in the harbour.

Kingstown from the East Pier. The card was posted in December 1904. A paddle steamer is at anchor in the harbour.

The town and harbour, Kingstown, c.1910. A mother and her children pose for the photographer against the backdrop of yachts moored in the harbour. On the left, is the lifeboat house and slipway, which was built in 1901. The station's first motor lifeboat was *Dunleary 1*, which came into service in 1919. Before this, the crews had to row the lifeboats, which also had small sails. However, even without motors, the crew of these lifeboats performed many heroic rescues in Dublin Bay. There were also lifeboat disasters, none more so than on Christmas Eve 1895 when the Kingstown no. 1 lifeboat (the *Civil Service No. 7*), going to the aid of a Russian ship, the *Palme*, was lost with all of her fifteen crew.

Kingstown Harbour showing yachts in Dublin Bay. The mail boats are berthed at Carlisle Pier. The railway cutting, with the bridges for pedestrians, runs parallel with the road. This card was posted in April 1913 to Brooklyn, New York, and the writer describes the harbour as 'the Gate of Ireland'.

Children on the East Pier at Kingstown, c.1920. It is early in the day so the bandstand is empty, but on most summer evenings, except Saturdays, a band would play for two hours. Steam rises from the funnels of the mail boat as it prepares to depart for Holyhead.

A photograph of the harbour in July 1907, showing two naval vessels with flags flying for the Royal Visit. This was the visit of King Edward VII and Queen Alexandra to Dublin for the International Exhibition at Herbert Park, Ballsbridge, on 10 July 1907.

An evening view of HMS *Melampus* at anchor in Kingstown Harbour. A Royal Navy guard ship was stationed in Kingstown Harbour until the early twentieth century. After this the Navy continued to use the harbour and the Atlantic Fleet visited in 1906 and 1907.

Harbour and East Pier, Dun Laoghaire, in the 1940s. The pier is crowded and the card shows a banner for a carnival on display in the harbour.

Davy Stevens selling newspapers on the East Pier. He was a familiar figure on the harbour with his thick overcoat, shiny shoes and moustache. The message on the card which is postmarked 4 April 1909 says, 'this is the man that sold me a newspaper on the quay today. Brown face, good appetite!'

The Mail Packet Station at Kingstown, c.1908. In the foreground is the monument to King George IV – a granite obelisk surmounted by a crown, which was erected by the Harbour Commissioners to commemorate the laying of the first stone of the harbour and the King's visit on 3 September 1821. The obelisk stood on four balls, which many felt was quite appropriate!

A busy scene at Carlisle Pier on a card postmarked 17 July 1930. The motor cars did not have access to the platform. The boat trains ran on to Carlisle Pier, which was a great advantage for rail passengers, who could board the boats directly.

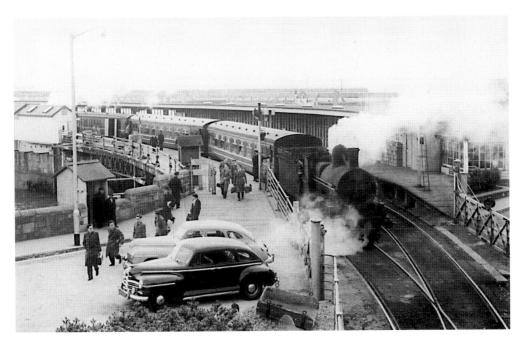

The boat train, *c.*1950. The train steams away from Carlisle Pier, passing through the level crossing, heading for Dublin. Some passengers walk to the waiting cars.

The classical façade of the clubhouse of the Royal St George Yacht Club, *c.*1915. This was designed by John Skipton Mulvaney and completed in 1843, but had to be extended the following year as the membership increased. It was one of the world's first 'purpose-built' yacht clubs and the interior layout has remained almost unchanged. The entrance hall has a domed skylight with a symbolic compass rose. Famous club members have included the Duke of Wellington in 1833 and Daniel O'Connell in 1846.

Victoria Parade, Kingstown, *c.*1905. The clubhouse of the Royal St George Yacht Club is on the left. Crowds gather near the Victoria Fountain. The elaborately decorated ironwork fountain was erected as a monument to Queen Victoria's visit in 1900. She had previously visited Ireland in 1849 and 1861. Davey Stevens is at the top of the steps in front of the fountain selling newspapers.

Davey Stevens, the Kingstown newsagent, *c.*1909. He was known as 'The King of Irish Newsagents'. He was always pictured with a paper in his hand and, on this occasion, he holds the *Daily Telegraph* for Thursday 27 May 1909, which reports that the King's horse Minoru was the winner of the Derby with a great popular ovation.

Victoria Road showing the Kingstown Pavilion, *c.*1904. The cutting for the railway can be seen on the right. An outside car pulled by a single horse heads down towards Victoria Road. People gather at the Victoria Fountain. The message on the card says that the 'Dandies' are performing at the Pavilion during the week.

The Town Hall and Courthouse, Kingstown, *c.*1907. Situated at the junction of Marine Road and Crofton Road, this is a two-storey building with a clock tower and has the appearance of a Venetian palace, with arched windows and coloured stonework. It was designed by J.L. Robinson and completed in 1880, at a cost of £16,000. There is a coloured window over the main entrance showing the Kingstown coat of arms (see p. 4). The cannon in the foreground came from the Crimea and was known by the townspeople as 'The Russian Trophy'.

The railway station and harbour, *c.*1912. The entrance to the Pavilion is in the foreground. On the left, can be seen the single storey neo-classical Station House, which was designed by J.S. Mulvaney and was built in 1845, costing £2,800. The platform has a large terminal shed with a high supporting wall. The construction of the wall was very impressive. It had an 'Italian- style' cornice at the top, on the side facing the harbour.

The railway station, Dun Laoghaire, *c.*1940. The Station House is seen at the end of the platform. The two men on the line (plate layers) are repairing a section of track.

Advertising card for Galligan's Luncheon and Tea Rooms at 115 Upper Georges Street, Kingstown, c.1910. Information is also presented that the rail journey from Westland Row to Kingstown takes only 15 minutes, or that one can have a delightful trip by electric tram from the City of Dublin for fourpence.

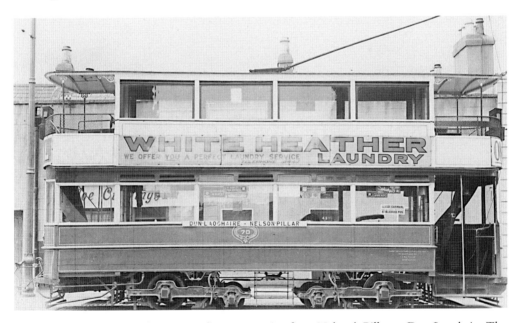

The electric tram, 1920s. There was a frequent service from Nelson's Pillar to Dun Laoghaire. The fare was much cheaper than the horse-drawn cab or motor cab. The advertisement on the side of the tram is for the White Heather Laundry, offering a 'perfect laundry service', which was situated at 2 Upper George's Street, Kingstown.

The Kingstown Pavilion, c.1907. There is a small queue outside the entrance to the Pavilion Gardens. The pavilion was designed by C. Owen and opened in 1903 by the Earl of Longford. It was like a large summerhouse and had a roof-top garden, a turret at each corner and various balconies and promenade walks. It was lit up at night by 'Electric Fairyland Illuminations' and was very popular, attracting large crowds for concerts, dances and variety shows. The pavilion was built using a lot of timber and unfortunately went on fire in November 1915. After this it was rebuilt, but then burnt down again in 1919. On this occasion, a horse from the Dublin fire brigade collapsed and died on arrival at the burning Pavilion. The replacement in the 1920s was a concrete structure and became the Pavilion Picture Theatre Cinema.

A charabanc or 'benched carriage' outside the entrance to the Pavilion Gardens, c.1907. The initials IMS on the vehicle stand for the Irish Motor Service Company, which started the service between Kingstown and Bray in 1905. The charabancs were specially built by the Albion Motor Company and used for excursions. The passengers were open to the elements, so most wore heavy coats.

The Central Hall of the Pavilion. This had a well-equipped stage, which was 35ft wide. The hall was surrounded by balconies, with flags and garlands. There was seating for 1,000 customers and the chairs could be removed for dances. The writer of the card, on 18 April 1905, says that on the previous Monday, he had been to the Pavilion and listened to a very good Viennese band.

A tea room at the Pavilion, showing the elaborate interior decoration and quality of the rooms. The service was of course 'waitress service' only and the writer of the card on 3 January 1905 says 'There's a girl wanted here!' Other rooms at the pavilion included smoking rooms and separate ladies' and gentlemen's reading rooms.

The Kingstown Pavilion roller-skating rink, *c.*1909. When the seats were removed, the auditorium was also used for the popular pastime of roller-skating. The pillars appear to be a hazard, and there must have been the occasional accident, but in those days a claim for personal injury against the owners would not have got very far!

A view of the harbour and both piers, showing the rear of the Kingstown Pavilion, taken from the Royal Marine Hotel, *c.*1913. The Town Hall is on the left and there is a large crowd in the pavilion gardens listening to the band. The gardens of the Royal Marine Hotel are fairly empty, but there are many people on the pavilion balconies enjoying the entertainment and viewing the harbour.

MARINE HOTEL, DUN LAOGHAIRE, KINGSTOWN

Above: The Royal Marine Hotel, Kingstown, *c.*1920. William Dargan bought the Royal Hotel on the site in 1863. The architect, John McCurdy, was asked to design a grand hotel of quality in keeping with the needs of Kingstown. The building was in the French renaissance style with a central tower and two wings. However, money ran short and, as a consequence, the eastern wing was completed but the western wing, which incorporated the old Royal Hotel, was left at a lower level. However, as the photograph shows, the two wings matched well, having similar windows, and the whole effect was that of a hotel of distinction. The interior was similar to an ornate château with very decorative rooms and ceilings. The gardens were laid out in terraces, with lawns, fountains and statues. There was also a bowling green.

Right: Tom, the luggage porter at the Royal Marine Hotel with Grip, his faithful companion, *c.*1910. They would meet hotel guests arriving by boat or train at Carlisle Pier.

Lower George's Street, Kingstown, *c.*1910. The Martello Towers at Dunleary Pier and Glasthule were built in 1805 and joined by a road for military movements. That straight road later became the basis for George's Street. The view shows the street crowded with carriages. The first shop on the left, at no. 90, is P.J. Hand, a confectioner.

A later view of Lower George's Street, *c.*1919. There are plenty of people in the town's main shopping street. On the left, at no. 86, is T. Brown, who sold tobacco, and the large shop after the junction with Sussex Street is Alex Findlater & Co., the traditional grocers and wine merchants. The projecting clock was a well-known landmark.

Lower George's Street, *c.*1910. A busy scene as an open-topped tram, bound for Dalkey, stops outside Findlaters to pick up passengers. Cyclists in the street needed to be very careful when riding on the cobbles and they also had to keep clear of the tramlines.

Lower George's Street, *c.*1910. An open-topped tram approaches the entrance to St Michael's church. Looking towards the camera is a constable from the Dublin Metropolitan Police, who wears a spiked helmet. On the front of the tram is an advertisement for umbrellas, which were sold by K. Johnston at 21 Nassau Street, Dublin.

Lower George's Street, Dun Laoghaire, *c.*1940. Tramcar no. 221 is outside the entrance to St Michael's church, closely followed by tramcar no. 185. Travellers wanting fresh air could sit on the front balcony of the trams, but most of the passengers on the upper deck were protected from the weather. The top windows of the trams had ventilators. The road surface was still cobbled.

Upper George's Street, Kingstown, *c.*1911. The street premises had a great variety of businesses including several doctors, solicitors and dentists. Some were multi-skilled and Coall, Talbot and Son, at no. 18, were estate agents, insurance agents, auctioneers, valuators and undertakers. They were prepared to cover every eventuality! An early motor car is parked on the right.

George's Street, Dunlaoghaire, Kingstown.

Upper George's Street, *c.*1930. P. McKeones, a provision warehouse, is the first shop on the left. On the opposite corner, is the Kingstown Picture House (nos 9-10), which opened in 1912 and seated 450 people. The cinema was very popular, although it was known to locals as the 'Bug House'. At that time, it was the place for magical popular entertainment for all ages, bringing dreams to life and, through newsreels, allowing people to see what was happening in the world. The programme changed twice a week. Every Sunday there was a double-bill and the 'serial'. In the 1930s, the name of the head usher was Drummond, whose nickname was 'Ace', called after the well-known hero, Ace Drummond.

Upper George's Street, Kingstown, *c.*1904. The two gentlemen on the right are standing in front of the Divisional Police Office (no. 100). The imposing building next door is the National Bank (nos 101–102).

St Mary's Dominican Convent, Kingstown, *c.*1904. Schoolgirls pose for the photographer in the gardens and in front of the ' Grotto' which has a statue of Our Lady. Many of the girls carry tennis racquets. In 1912, the convent had forty-five nuns, fifty boarders and eighty day pupils. The St Mary's Convent National School, also run by the Dominican Nuns at Echo Lodge, was larger and had 1,060 pupils.

Clarinda Park School, *c.*1906. The school was at the end of a terrace at no. 18 Clarinda Park East. It had a classical porch with a lion crowning the entrance. On the same road was Victoria School at no. 23 (which later became Glengara Park School). The development at Clarinda Park, by Mr P.W. Bryan, a wealthy wine merchant, took place around 1850 in the grounds of Stoneview House. The Clarinda Park grounds were used for school sports. There was a good tennis club and in 1890, the annual fee to use the courts was three guineas. However, fees at the nearby Crosthwaite Park tennis club were only one guinea per year.

Crosthwaite Park West, Kingstown, c.1905. John Crosthwaite developed the square in 1860. The west side terrace, pictured here, had houses with large bay windows extending up two storeys. The front doors were paired and residents shared wide steps. The interiors were ornate and rooms had white marble fireplaces with ornamental plaster work on the ceilings. The writer of this card says the photograph appears to have been taken at midnight as all the blinds are down! Around 1890, the playwright, John Millington Synge, author of *Playboy of the Western World* lived at no. 29 Crosthwaite Park West. In 1894, he proposed marriage to Cherrie Matheson, who lived at no. 25 but, after she turned him down, he went to Paris.

Rosmeen Gardens, Kingstown, c.1912. This row of Edwardian-style, red-brick semi-detached houses was built in the grounds of Granite Hall in 1905/06. Both Granite Hall and Stoneview House (see opposite page, Clarinda Park) were magnificent houses built in the 1820s by George Smyth, the stone contractor for the Kingstown Harbour. The houses in Rosmeen Gardens were certainly more modest, but in 1912, William George, the Portuguese Consul, was living at no. 7.

St Michael's Hospital, Lower George's Street, Kingstown, c.1912. The hospital was built of grey Dalkey granite in a similar style to the Town Hall. It cost £6,000 and was opened in 1876. The Sisters of Mercy ran the hospital, which was dependent on voluntary contributions from the public. In 1912, the hospital had fifty beds and a large dispensary.

Victoria House Hotel, Victoria Terrace, Kingstown, c.1905. The hotel was formed by the amalgamation of two houses, which had been built on the waterfront by Thomas Egan in 1843. The proprietor was Thomas Ross and Ross's Hotel was very popular. In the 1930s it had an 'electric lift' and an added attraction was the 'winter garden' on the hotel roof.

The People's Gardens, Kingstown, *c.*1905. This public park was laid out on a site of five acres by J.L. Robinson, who also designed the Town Hall. Previously, this was the location of Glasthule Martello Tower. However, the tower was demolished around 1889. The park opened in 1890 and had formal gardens with two iron fountains, a bandstand and a great view over Dublin Bay.

The writer of the card says they are motoring near Dun Laoghaire on 3 July 1927. It looks a good day. The starting handle on the front of the car brings back memories!

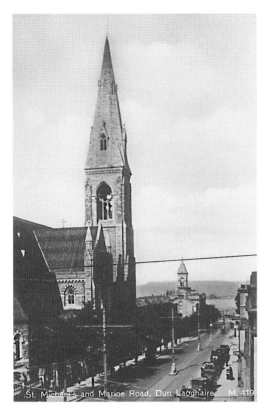

St. Michael's and Marine Road, Dun Laoghaire.   M. 419.

St Michael's church and Marine Road, Dun Laoghaire, c.1920. Around 1820, there was a simple church building in the form of a cross. The replacement, built in the 1870s, was this fine Gothic church built to the plans of C.J. McCarthy, known as 'the Irish Pugin', who had also designed Armagh Cathedral. Unfortunately, the church was destroyed by fire in 1968. The magnificent spire is the only part of the old church which survives in the present building.

The chancel of St Michael's church, Dun Laoghaire, c.1920. It had a most elaborate decorated appearance. There were fine murals on the walls and lots of inlaid marble. Mr John Crosthwaite, the developer of Crosthwaite Park (see p. 69), paid for the beautiful stained-glass east window behind the altar.

St Joseph's church, Glasthule, Dun Laoghaire, *c.*1925. The church was designed by Pugin and Ashlin and built in 1867 in the French Gothic style. It had two matching turrets and a fine rose window seen above the entrance. The church is similar in style to St Patrick's church at Monkstown (see p. 46).

The wedding of Margaret Farrell and Kevin Mullen at St Joseph's church, Glasthule, on 28 August 1950. The church was well known for its fine altar and white statues.

Fairground at Dun Laoghaire in the 1950s. A busy scene with a packed merry-go-round and people queuing for ice cream. Regular small fairs were held on St Michael's Wharf, in the shadow of the mail boat, until the mid-1960s.

The Promenade, Dun Laoghaire, in the 1950s. People enjoy the views of the mail boat and the harbour.

The beach and Children's Bathing Place, Kingstown, c.1918. The rather rocky beach was approached by steep, winding steps. Several nurse-maids with prams sit on the benches. From the 1830s onwards, rows of fine terraced houses were built along the seafront.

The Baths, Dun Laoghaire, c.1930. In 1843, John Crosthwaite built the Royal Victoria Baths at the corner of Scotsman's Bay. Customers could bathe in the open sea, or in the outdoor baths. They could also have individual reclining baths, which were recommended by the medical profession for rheumatism, sciatica and lumbago. There was a good choice as the selection included hot or cold sea-water baths, hot fresh-water baths, special seaweed baths and Russian steam baths. The baths were a very popular attraction for visitors and residents. The Kingstown Town Council bought the baths and completely rebuilt them around 1910.

The Baths, Dun Laoghaire, c.1930. This view shows the main pool and buildings from the seaward side. There were no diving boards. The writer of the card, on holiday from Liverpool, comments on the beautiful scenery and says that she goes swimming in the baths every morning, between 8 and 8.30 a.m.

The children's paddling pool at the Baths, Dun Laoghaire, c.1930. Children, wearing the bathing costumes of the day, play happily in the small pool. In the distance, boats are seen in the harbour.

Six

The Ferries

An advertising postcard for the London and North Western Railway company, *c.*1905. The railway company was based at Holyhead. The Irish Mail contract was secured by the Royal City of Dublin Steam Packet Company in 1849, causing rivalry between the two companies which was to last for seventy years. Before the First World War, the LNWR had four express steamers based at Holyhead, the *Cambria* (1897), *Anglia* (1900), *Hibernia* (1900) and *Scotia* (1902). There was a daylight passenger service between Holyhead and Dun Laoghaire which took about five hours and a night service to Dublin North Wall. The *Cambria* and *Scotia* survived the war, but the *Hibernia* (renamed as HMS *Tara*) was sunk in the Mediterranean on 5 November 1915 by a German submarine, and the *Anglia* was sunk by a mine on 17 November 1915. In 1920, the railway company was again awarded the mail contract and introduced four new ships to the Holyhead-Dun Laoghaire route.

Departure of Mail Boat, Kingstown

The mail boat RMS *Leinster* departing from Dun Laoghaire, *c.*1916. This was one of the four vessels (*Ulster, Munster, Leinster* and *Connaught*) commissioned by the City of Dublin Steam Packet Company in 1896. They took only three hours to sail between Holyhead and Dun Laoghaire. The mail boats continued to sail during the First World War and on 10 October 1918, a month before the end of the war, the *Leinster* was torpedoed by a German submarine near the Kish Lightship, about sixteen miles out from Kingstown. She had 687 passengers and a crew of 70. She sank quickly and although the destroyers *Lively* and *Mallard* went to her aid, rescue work was hindered by high seas. Some 501 lives were lost including that of Captain Birch. Most of the survivors were taken to the hospital at Kingstown.

The Royal Mail boat SS *Ulster*, sister ship of RMS *Leinster*, steams away from Kingstown for Holyhead, *c.*1915. She could sail at a speed of 24 knots and gave a fast, reliable service. During the war she had several narrow escapes, including being hit by a torpedo which failed to explode on 23 October 1918. After the war, the City of Dublin Company lost the mail contract and the *Munster* carried the mails from Holyhead to Kingstown for the last time on 27 November 1927. It was the end of an era, for the company had operated the Irish Mail services very successfully with speed, punctuality and reliability for seventy years.

In 1920/21, after regaining the mail contract, the London, Midland and Scottish Railway introduced four new ships, built by Dennys of Dumbarton, to the Holyhead-Dun Laoghaire route. These were the *Anglia* (1920), *Hibernia* (1920), *Scotia* (1921) and *Cambria* (1921). They could sail at 25 knots, taking about three hours to make the crossing.

The captain on the Promenade Deck of SS *Scotia*, c.1925. The ship had twin funnels and large cowl ventilators. The forward end of the open promenade deck was enclosed using glass windows when she had a refit in 1932. On 1 June 1940, during the Second World War, the ship was lost with most of her crew at Dunkirk.

The first-class dining saloon on SS *Cambria*. This was on the forward main deck, below the cabins on the promenade deck. The standards were high and passengers had 'silver service' and individual attention from the waiters. First-class accommodation on the ship included a selection of cabins and berths and a smoking room. The lounge had luxurious armchairs, sofas and a 'coal-effect' electric fire. However, standards in the third-class accommodation were very basic.

The mail boat *Hibernia* and lifeboat at Dun Laoghaire, *c*.1958. The RMS *Hibernia* and her sister ship the *Cambria* were built by Harland and Wolff at Belfast. They both came into service in 1949 and continued on the route until 1974. They carried around 2,000 passengers and were virtually one class ships, as they had only a small amount of first-class accommodation.

Seven

People and Events

The Royal Visit, July 1903. Cheering crowds line the way as King Edward VII and Queen Alexandra, in the Royal carriage, pass through Crofton Road, Kingstown.

The Royal Visit to Dublin on 8 July 1911. King George V and Queen Mary in the Royal Barge are seen approaching the wharf at Kingstown.

Kingstown Harbour, showing the Royal Yacht and the landing of Their Majesties on 8 July 1911. There were twenty-three warships of the Home Fleet in Kingstown Harbour for the visit.

The first Dáil: Eamon de Valera was chosen as President after Cathal Brugha stepped down on 1 April 1919. This group photograph taken in Dublin is dated 10 April 1919. From left to right, front row: L. Ginnell, Michael Collins (leader of the Irish Republican Army), Cathal Brugha, Arthur Griffith (founder of Sinn Féin), Eamon de Valera (President), Count Plunkett, E. MacNeill, William Cosgrave, E. Blythe. Second row: P. Maloney, T. McSwiney (Lord Mayor of Cork), Richard Mulcahy, J. O'Doherty, J. O'Mahony, J. Dolan, J. McGuinness, P. O'Keefe, M. Staines, S. McGrath, B. Cussack, L. de Roiste, W. Coliver, Fr Michael Flanagan. Third row: P. War, A. McCabe, D. Fitzgerald, J. Sweeney, R. Hayes, G. Collins, P. O'Maillie, J. O'Mara, B. O'Higgins, J. Burke, K. O'Higgins. Fourth row: J. McDonagh, J. McEntee. Fifth row: P. Beasely, R. Dartan, P. Galligan. Sixth row: P. Shanahan, S. Etchingham.

Irish Peace Conference in July 1921. Following the Anglo-Irish truce, a delegation led by Eamon de Valera went to London for meetings with Lloyd George. Some of the delegates are shown leaving Dun Laoghaire, from left to right: Arthur Griffith, Robert Barton, Eamon de Valera, Count Plunkett and Laurence O'Neill. The delegation arrived in London on 12 July and met Lloyd George for the first meeting at Downing Street on 14 July. Unfortunately, the negotiations were not successful. Further meetings were held before a treaty which established the Irish Free State was signed, by a different Irish delegation, on 6 December 1921. The historic consequences which followed are well known.

Eucharistic Congress, Dublin, 1932. The Papal Legate, Cardinal Lorenzo Lauri, arrived at Dun Laoghaire on 20 June 1932 for the thirty-first International Eucharistic Congress, which was organized by the Catholic Church to promote devotion to the Blessed Sacrament. He received a great welcome and is seen here with President de Valera, blessing the Guard of Honour at Carlisle Pier.

Dutch Girl Guides at Blackrock College during the Dublin Eucharistic Congress, 22-26 June 1932. Pilgrims came from all over the world and Blackrock College was the base for this large group. The city was packed for the Congress and seven ocean liners moored in Dublin Port were used to provide extra accommodation.

A photograph of a side-car taken in the South Dublin area in summer 1922. The message on the card, which was posted from Dublin to Chicago, on 9 August 1922, says that the passengers are Howard Valentine and his son, Patrick, sitting on an 'Irish Ford'.

Ernest Shackleton, the Antarctic explorer, was born at Kilkea, Co. Kildare on 15 February 1874. The family moved to 35 Marlborough Road, Donnybrook, when he was six years old, as his father came to Trinity to study medicine. As a boy, he was fascinated by the sea and would watch the boats at Dublin Docks and from Kingstown Pier. He left Ireland when his father joined a medical practice at Sydenham. However, he never lost his love of the sea and was a merchant seaman before joining Captain Scott's expedition of 1901. He led his own Antarctic expedition, almost reaching the South Pole in 1907. In 1914, showing great daring, he successfully led an expedition which crossed the mountains of the Antarctic. Unfortunately, on a further expedition in 1922 he died suddenly from a heart attack. He was buried in South Georgia on 5 January 1922.

E.H. SHACKLETON. C.V.O.   PHOTO BY BERESFORD.

The victorious Teachers' Choir with their trophy at Dun Laoghaire Town Hall in March 1949.

The members of Ballybrack Irish Country Women's Association Choir with their conductor, Vera Byrne.

Members of Our Lady's Musical Society, Sallynoggin, who appeared in *Naughty Marietta* in 1978.

Members of Our Lady's Musical Society, Sallynoggin, who appeared in Grizett's *Merry Widow* in 1980.

Motorcyclists racing on a grass track at the sports grounds in Rochestown Avenue, Sallynoggin in May 1956.

An enthusiastic group of motorcyclists gather at Terenure College sports fields in July 1956. The rider of the bike with number 16 was Stan Brooks from Blackrock.

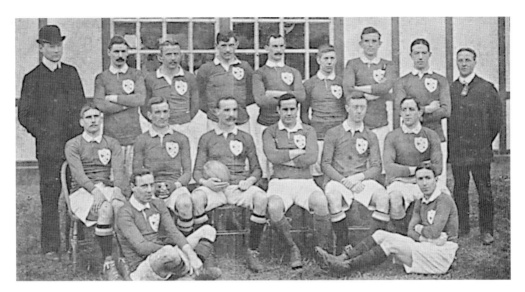

The Irish rugby football team which triumphed over England by 16 points to 6, in 1905. From left to right, back row: J.R. Moffatt, Lt. B. MacLear, H.G. Wilson, H.J. Knox, H. Thrift, G. Hamlet, J.J. Coffey. Middle row: A.D. Harvey, M.F. Landers, C.E. Allen, A. Tedford, J. Wallace, H.J. Miller. Front row: T.H. Robinson, E.D. Cadell.

The Irish Free State soccer team, which defeated the USA 3-1 in Dublin on 16 June 1924. From left to right, back row: D. Smith, C. Dowdall, P. Gilhooley, W. Burke, M. Murphy, J.S. Murphy. Middle row: G. Byrne, M. Foley, J. O'Sullivan, A. Kirkland, F. Collins, F. Brady, E. Marlowe, C. Harris (Trainer), T. Gough. Front row: J.J. Dunne, P. Robinson, J. Leonard, P. McEvoy (president), R. Fullam (captain), E. Brooks, P. O'Brien, J.L. Brennan, Capt. A.J. Prince-Cox (Referee). Both teams had competed in the 1924 Olympics in Paris, where the Irish team had progressed to the quarter-finals before being beaten 2-1 in extra time by the Netherlands.

Roger Casement was born at Doyle's Cottage, 29 Lawson Terrace, Sandycove Road on 1 September 1864. His mother died when he was nine and he went to live with his uncle at Ballycastle. He joined the British Consular service in 1892 and gained international recognition for exposing human rights abuses in the treatment of rubber plantation workers in Peru. He joined the Irish Volunteers in 1913. He was active in Germany and obtained weapons to help the Rebellion. However, after landing from a German U-boat on Banna Strand in Tralee Bay on 21 April 1916 he was arrested for attempting to bring the weapons into Ireland. He was tried for treason after the Easter Rising and hanged on 3 August 1916. His remains were interred in Glasnevin Cemetery in 1965.

Eamon De Valera was born in New York in 1882. When aged three, he came to Limerick where he grew up. He was educated at Blackrock College and University College, Dublin. He became a mathematician and taught at Carysfort Training College, Blackrock. He married his Irish teacher, Sinead Flanagan, in 1910 and they lived in Donnybrook. During the 1916 Rebellion he commanded the forces at Boland's Mills. He was sentenced to death but reprieved. A year later, he was elected President of Sinn Féin, but this was followed by some years in which he had periods of imprisonment. In 1924, he founded the Fianna Fáil party, which came to power in 1932 with himself as Taoiseach. From 1933, he lived at various addresses in Blackrock, moving to Cross Avenue in 1940. He was president of Ireland from 1959 to 1973. His retirement was spent at Talbot Lodge, Blackrock, until his death in 1975.

Eight

Sandycove, Dalkey and Killiney

Sandycove, County Dublin, *c.*1950. The Martello Tower at Sandycove Point is on the right. James Joyce stayed here with Oliver St John Gogarty for six days in September 1904. The visit was short, tempestuous and memorable. The opening scene of *Ulysses* takes place at the gun platform on the roof of this Martello Tower. In 1964, the tower became a Joycean museum.

The Forty Foot, Sandycove, c.1920. At Sandymount Point, between the Martello Tower and the Forty Foot bathing place, was a battery or fort, which held a small garrison of thirty-six artillery men. In the early nineteenth century, the place was called the 'Forty Foot Hole', as it had deep water and good fishing, although some claim it was named after the Fortieth Foot Regiment, who were stationed for a time at the Battery and Martello Tower. By tradition, in Victorian times sexes were segregated and the bathing was for 'gentlemen only'. It was just towards the end of the twentieth century that ladies began using the Forty Foot.

The Main Street, Sandycove, c.1920. A quiet scene with a variety of shops including a grocer, a dairy, a builder, a shoemaker and the post-office.

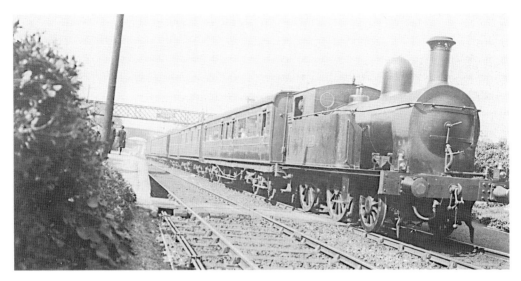

The Dublin to Bray train (Great Southern Railway, no. 428) at Dalkey station during September 1929. The station was originally the terminus of an experimental 'atmospheric railway' from Kingstown, which opened in 1844. The trains were sucked along by a vacuum using power from the Dalkey engine house. However, the venture was not a success and the Dalkey line was converted to conventional haulage with steam trains in 1854.

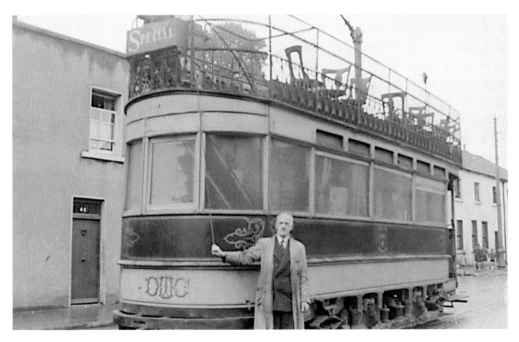

The Dublin United Tramways director's car at Dalkey, *c.*1930. This special tram, which had no number, was used by the directors of the Dublin United Tramways on official business. It was built at the Dublin United Tramways Company works at Spa Road, Inchicore, in 1901 and fitted out by Clery's of Dublin. The tram had velvet covered oak swivel seats, a writing bureau, Waterford glass lamps and a cocktail cabinet in the saloon. As all of the directors were gentlemen, it did not have the usual decency screen on the upper deck, but had a special wrought iron railing.

Dalkey from Sorrento Park, showing Killiney Hill in the distance and Vico Road, *c.*1903. Dame Blanche MacDonnell, who lived at Sorrento Cottage, gave the park for the benefit of residents in 1894. There was a Dalkey Amusements Committee, which arranged entertainment in the area and managed the park. The bandstand with its ornamental lighting is seen in the centre. Dalkey was renowned for the purity of its air and was a favourite summer resort of many of the leading Dublin doctors including Sir Dominic Corrigan, who lived at Inniscorrig.

Sorrento Terrace and Dalkey Island, *c.*1908. The grand terrace of eight houses, designed by Frederick Darley and Nathaniel Montgomery, was built in this exclusive position by Edward Masterton of Georges Street, Kingstown in 1845. The terrace had a boat slip and bathing place. Regattas were held off Sorrento Point in the 1890s.

Bullock Castle, Dalkey, c.1935. This view shows the medieval castle and the adjacent house built around 1720. The castle overlooks Bullock Harbour and creek. It was built around 1150 by the Cistercian Monks of St Mary's Abbey in the City to guard their fisheries. The fishermen would pay a toll to the monks for fishing in the harbour. The castle also provided board and lodging for travellers. The monks stayed there for over 400 years, until the time of Henry VIII.

Dalkey Island from Coliemore Harbour, c.1935. The harbour has two small piers and was built in 1868/69 by John Cunningham from 21 Ardeevin Road, Dalkey. As one rowing boat leaves, more visitors wait to board the next boat for Dalkey Island. Only goats and birds live on the seventeen-acre island. However, people would visit the ruins of St Begnet's early Christian church, which can just be seen in the centre of the island and the Martello Tower, built in 1804, which is on the right.

An early view of Castle Street, Dalkey, *c.*1905. Dalkey was a port in Norman times and was once known as the town of seven castles. Two of these, the Goat Castle and Archbold's Castle, still survive in the Main Street along with St Begnet's church. This was a charming old village with a single main street of shops. The Medical Hall, a pharmaceutical chemist, is on the right at no. 23.

Castle Street, Dalkey, *c.*1915. The Goat Castle, on the right, which was owned by the Cheevers family in the sixteenth century, became the Dalkey Town Hall in 1869. On the pavement on the left, a gentleman passes by Doherty & Co., a general drapers and outfitters shop at no. 47. The tramlines, taking the sweep across Castle Street to the right, are crossing into the tramyard.

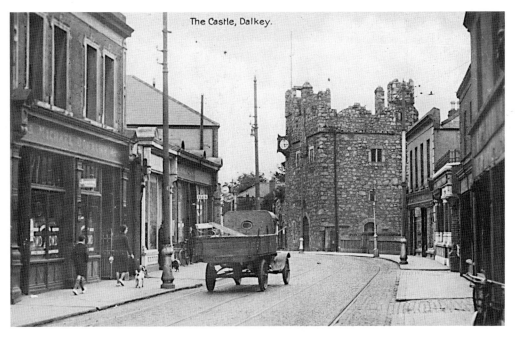

The Castle, Dalkey.

Castle Street, Dalkey, *c.*1930. An early-morning scene showing a lorry driving with solid-looking tyres on the road. It has just driven past Michael Donachy, wine and spirit merchant, on the left.

Castle Street, Dalkey.

Castle Street, Dalkey, *c.*1940. The tramcar has stopped at the terminus outside the offices of the Dublin United Tramways Company. For many years, trams provided a popular, efficient service taking around fifty minutes for the nine-mile journey between Nelson's Pillar and Dalkey. However, as other forms of transport attracted more passengers, trams became less profitable and the last Dalkey tram ran in July 1949. The Dalkey Public Library is on the right.

Dalkey Quarry, *c.*1925. The quarry at Dalkey Hill opened in 1815 to supply granite for the building of the harbour at Dun Laoghaire. Over 600 men worked on the harbour project and the quarried stone was taken in trucks to the harbour by way of a small railway on a track called 'The Metals'. The windmill on the right, which was used to pump water to the fields and nearby cottages, stands on the old Metals track.

Castle Park, Dalkey, *c.*1904. Around 1815, this was the most important house between Dalkey and Sandycove. In 1830, Alderman Arthur Perrin enlarged the house by building a striking mock-Tudor mansion with battlements facing the sea. In 1904, Mr W.P. Toone opened the Castle Park School in the mansion. It attracted many pupils from abroad. The sender of the card, to Rugby in England, writes that this is the back of the school and he has rooms in the tower on the right. He likes Ireland, as 'the people are so good and kind'.

Above: A family scene on a postcard sent from Redan House, Dalkey, postmarked 2 July 1905. Children pose with their pets for the photographer. The goat and cart take pride of place, while the rabbit and the dog look on. The boy looks very smart, wearing a sailor suit, which was an attractive form of dress for young people who admired the bravery and exploits of sea heroes of the time.

Leftt: A photograph of a mother and son at Dalkey on a card dated 15 September 1906.

Cliff Castle Hotel, Dalkey, *c.*1925. The mock-medieval castle was designed by McCurdy and Mitchell. It was built in a superb situation with battlements on the terraces, which led to a private harbour. It became a hotel in the 1920s.

The Loreto Convent, Dalkey, *c.*1907. This was an imposing convent built in the form of a cross in 1842 and situated in a splendid position overlooking the sea. It had a private bathing place, which was for women only. The Loreto nuns opened a private boarding school and in 1912, there were thirty-three nuns at the convent, which had fifty-four girls as boarders. They also ran the Convent National School, which had 250 pupils.

Seafield Road, Killiney, *c.*1930. The houses on the road were developed around 1850 by William Field, who was a grocer in Ballybrack. There were superb views from the road over Killiney Beach and Dublin Bay. At this point, the railway line runs parallel with the road. The train is steaming towards Bray.

Killiney from the railway, 1940s. Killiney Hill and its obelisk can be seen in the background. Fine houses and villas overlooking Killiney beach are dotted on the hillside. At that time, the coast road was narrow, but there was not a lot of traffic. Cars could drive fairly safely in the centre of the road, drawing to the side if meeting another car. However, the nursemaid sensibly walks on the pavement, as she takes her child out in a pushchair.

A quiet scene at Killiney station, *c*.1925. The strand is also deserted. The mansions stand out among the trees on Killiney Hill. The corrugated roof of the footbridge crossing the line has been blackened by smoke from the trains.

Interior of Killiney station, *c*.1933. After leaving the station, a train steams around the curve of the Bay towards Dun Laoghaire. Passengers standing on the platform on the left are talking to the guard.

Holidaymakers on Killiney Strand, looking towards Killiney Hill, c.1930. The boats on the beach were rented out to tourists and fishermen. Around 1750, there was an unsuccessful attempt to mine for lead and silver at Killiney. It is interesting that, from time to time, small garnets have been found among the sands of Killiney Strand.

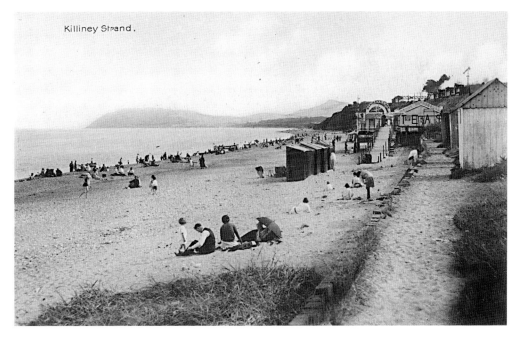

The view from the opposite end of the Strand, looking towards Bray Head, c.1930. Children play on the sands. There are bathing huts in the centre of the beach. On the right, past the tea bar, with the curved sign, is Stanley's Café.

The White Cottage, Killiney, c. 1930. This was built as a summerhouse and tea rooms. The Homan family lived in the cottage. In 1923, they successfully ran dances on a platform on the beach. However, the weather was not always the best, so in 1924, they built the indoor ballroom, standing on pillars, shown in the photograph. The popular tea dances were from 8 p.m. to midnight every Saturday and Sunday. In fact, the banner hanging on the side of the house is advertising a 'dance tonight'. The chalets at the side of the cottage, on the left, were let to holiday makers. M. Homan, the sender of the card, writes to a girl in Liverpool that she can have accommodation if she is prepared to share with two other young ladies from London. He says they all have separate beds!

The Monument, Killiney Hill, 1950s. The winter of 1741/42 was very severe and caused much hardship among the poor and the working class. John Malpas, a wealthy landowner, decide to build an obelisk on Killiney Hill, in order to provide some work for the unemployed. It was intended to form the centrepiece of gardens on the hill. The obelisk was over 500 feet above sea level and had a viewing balcony. It attracted many visitors, who would come to admire the views of the coast and Wicklow mountains – certainly a view to compare with the Bay of Naples. Killiney Hill Park was laid out as Victoria Park in 1887 to celebrate the fiftieth year of the Queen's reign, and remains a popular public park.

Killiney Castle Hotel, *c.*1950. The was originally called 'Mount Malpas' after Colonel John Malpas, who built the house in 1740. It has had many owners since, who have made various changes, but it was Robert Warren, in 1840, who added the mock medieval corner towers, turrets and battlements. The tower entrance and doorway was built by Thomas Higgin in 1872.

Young ladies from the Sion Hill Convent (see p. 39) at the Debutante Dance at Killiney Castle Hotel on Friday 23 October 1977.

Above:: Dorset Lodge, Killiney, *c.*1904. The house was built in the early part of the nineteenth century on the Military Road. It was named after the fourth Duke of Dorset who died after falling from his horse at the age of twenty-two years while out hunting in Killiney. Various extensions to the house have been added over the years.

Left: Maureen O'Sullivan in 1948. Just one of the many famous stars who has lived in Killiney. She played Jane in the series of Tarzan films with Johnny Weismuller and also starred with Count John McCormack in *Song of my Heart* in 1930. Her daughter is Mia Farrow.

Nine

Bray and Greystones

The Cliff Walk, *c*.1905. This is a magnificent walk along the cliffs for about five miles from Bray down to Greystones. Below the path can be seen the railway running through tunnels carved from the rock, with a steep drop down to the deep green sea. The design for the railway line along the sea cliffs was by Brunel and building the track around 1850 proved a difficult feat of engineering, needing several tunnels and viaducts. The Cliff Walk, or 'Railway Walk', started above Bray Cove Baths and, due to the breathtaking views, was always very popular. At that time, as can be seen in the photograph, ladies had to dress very formally when out walking.

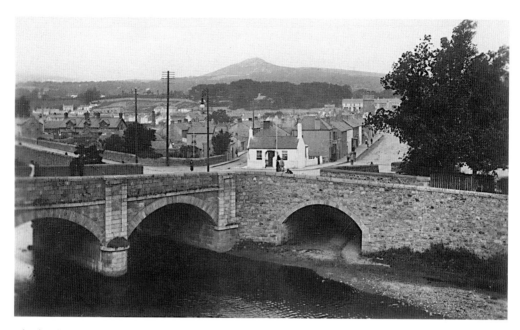

The bridge over the River Dargle and Little Bray, c.1903. The bridge, at the entrance to the town, was built by David Edge in 1856. At that time, Little Bray had a mainly working-class population. The houses were mainly thatched, single-storey cottages. Living conditions were poor and there were no adequate sewers. It is not surprising that there were several cholera and smallpox epidemics in Little Bray. In 1904, due to poverty, overcrowding and damp conditions, there was said to be one in eight people in the area suffering from tuberculosis.

Ravenswell Row, Little Bray, on 26 August 1905. Minor flooding from the River Dargle was not uncommon. However, in August 1905, the river burst its banks and there was a disastrous flood in Little Bray. There was much damage to property and about 2,000 people were made homeless. They were given temporary accommodation in the Town Hall, the Royal Hotel and the Sunnybank Inn. Many people had to be rescued from the floods, but only one person, a Mr James Plunkett, was drowned.

Sheridan's Lane, Little Bray, 26 August 1905. The wall is marked to the height reached by the floodwaters, which looks to be about five feet. There are grim expressions on the faces of those who have been made homeless. After the floods there was an appeal by Lord Meath for donations to help the victims of the flood, which met with a generous response.

Dargle Road and the Cripples' Home, Little Bray, 26 August 1905. The Cripples' Home had been founded by Lucinda Sullivan in 1874 and was entirely dependent upon voluntary support. The home gave shelter to any poor and homeless crippled children, whenever there were beds available and funds allowed. The flood was a disaster for the home.

Little Bray on 25 August 1905. Carriages were abandoned during the floods as floodwaters reached heights of six to eleven feet.

Little Bray on 25 August 1905. Total devastation was caused as walls and buildings were washed away by the floodwaters. The effects of the disaster were worsened as this was a deprived area, where there was overcrowding in houses and inadequate plumbing and sanitation.

Photograph by 'Harrison' of some of those people who risked their lives in saving others during the floods in Little Bray on the night of 25 August 1905. It is a tribute to the rescuers that there was so little loss of life.

A further study by 'Montgomery for Killick of Bray', showing some of the heroes and heroines of the disastrous floods in Bray on 26 August 1905. Compared with the photograph by Harrison, this group shows some additional heroes and also includes ladies.

Bray Head and the Esplanade, *c*.1905. The sea wall and Promenade were built in 1886, when Bray was considered the 'Brighton of Ireland'. This photograph, by Killick, shows many 'well-to-do' visitors strolling on the promenade. The Bray Amusements Committee, which had been formed in 1875, arranged for entertainment on the Bandstand. During the summer months, three different military bands would play there each week. The bands could use the railway to come to Bray free of charge. When the weather was bad, the bands would play on the railway platform (see p. 115). Suggested plans for a Bray Pier, similar to that at Brighton, never came to fruition.

The Promenade Strand, Bray, *c*.1935. By this time, Bray had become less exclusive and was more of a pleasure resort. The photograph shows the beach crowded with holidaymakers. William's Amusement Park can be seen at Bray Head.

The Esplanade, Bray, with crowds watching the 'White Coons', who are appearing on the bandstand, c.1908. Entertainment was organised by the Bray Amusement Committee and another popular show that appeared regularly on the bandstand, was 'George Rapley's Troupe'. The Esplanade Hotel and Lacy's Hotel are on the right.

Photograph by Killick of Will C. Pepper's 'White Coons' at Bray in 1909. They sang in harmony and were very popular. The group would need a different name today!

The Boat Slip, Bray

The Boat Slip, Bray, c.1920. Children play happily on the beach against the background of Bray Head.

THE BATHS AT BRAY HEAD   R 1993

The open air baths at Bray Head on a busy summer's day, c.1950. The baths were popular attraction for many years and until the 1930s there were separate male and female bathing areas.

Carriages wait at the attractive Bray railway station, c.1908. The first railway arrived at Bray in July 1854. By giving easy, fast travel from Dublin or the boats at Kingstown, the railway brought many new visitors to Bray. It was a busy and profitable line and excursion trains were crowded with tourists and commuters. The station was ideally situated for the town and promenade.

Interior of Bray railway station, c.1946. The station has broad extensive platforms on each side, with large covered areas for waiting passengers. In bad weather, the bands booked for the bandstand on the Promenade, or the gardens at the Marine Hotel, would play on the platforms at the railway station. The platform on the left, which was built in 1927, has a large glass canopy. Local rail staff called this the 'Crystal Palace'. The locomotive in the foreground has stopped to take on water.

A busy scene on the Main Street, Bray, c.1915. The building with the flag on the left is the Royal Hotel. On the right is William Porter's carriage factory, at no. 112, which is next to the Hibernian Bank. The tower of the Holy Redeemer church is seen behind the bank. In 1915, the street had all the usual mix of businesses, including Findlaters at no. 17. However, there were also several hairdressers, a pawnbroker at no. 38 and a bootmaker at no. 39.

Quinsboro Road, Bray, c.1915. St Andrew's Presbyterian church, which opened in 1858, is on the left. At that time, the street had a wide range of shops including jewellers, milliners, wine merchants and tobacconists. In addition, there were several doctors, a dentist and a solicitor in the side terraces. The shop on the right belongs to Miss Anna Gethings, who sold stationery and fancy goods.

Florence Road, Bray, *c.*1910. A typical terraced road in the more affluent part of Bray. The Holy Redeemer church is facing the end of the road.

The Marine Station Hotel, Strand Road, Bray, *c.*1914. The Royal Marine Hotel was built in 1855 by Edward Breslin, a friend of William Dargan. He also built the exclusive Brennan Terrace and was to become one of the largest landowners in the town. William Dargan realized Bray's potential as a fashionable seaside resort. He developed the promenade and built Turkish baths, which opened in 1859. The Royal Marine Hotel was purchased, in 1912, by the Dublin and South Eastern Railway. They carried out improvements, fitted electric light and then renamed it the Marine Station Hotel.

The Princess Patricia Hospital, Bray, c. 1915. During the First World War, in early 1915, the rooms in the International Hotel, Bray were converted into bedded wards and the hotel was used as a Red Cross Military Hospital for wounded troops. Red Cross nurses and members of the St. John's Ambulance Association helped staff the hospital. Ladies from Christ Church parish also helped by making surgical dressings and doing voluntary work at the hospital. Soldiers were sent from the Dublin hospitals for convalescence. The hospital was initially used for fitting artificial limbs. However, in 1916, the Meath Industrial School for Girls closed and was taken over by the Red Cross. They reopened it as the Duke of Connaught's Hospital for the fitting of artificial limbs. The Princess Patricia Hospital was then used solely for soldiers to recover their strength and normal health after injury.

The County Wicklow Ward, Princess Hospital, Bray, c. 1915. This is the converted hotel ballroom and appears very well staffed. A soldier playing a ukulele sits in the centre of the ward. The Hospital did have a small band formed by the soldiers and this group, called the 'Blue Boys', would give concerts for the other patients. The writer of the card, who is a patient in the ward, says there is a lot of snow on the hills, which look very pretty and remind him of Dartmoor!

The tennis and croquet grounds, Princess Patricia Hospital, Bray, *c.*1915. Sporting activities were encouraged during convalescence. The soldiers are wearing uniforms to play tennis and croquet, and there are plenty of spectators! The hospital also had a cricket team, which played regularly against Aravon School on the Meath Road. This school had two very distinguished past pupils in Roger Casement and John Millington Synge.

The Band of the 87th Royal Irish Fusiliers (Faugh-a-Ballaghs). They were a prize-winning band who played at the bandstand on the promenade and also in the gardens at the Royal Marine Hotel (see p. 112).

A group from the Fellowship Holiday Association staying in Bray in Summer 1957.

Bray Town Choir, looking very smart, c.1980.

The Royal Hotel, Main Street, Bray, *c.*1950.

A happy group of young people, including some footballers from Shamrock Rovers, at a dinner dance at the Royal Hotel, Bray, in January 1966.

The aerial chair-lift rope-way to the Eagle's Nest, Bray, *c.*1953. The chair-lift was built in 1950 by Eamonn Quinn, who also owned Red Island Holiday Camp at Skerries. This was a new venture in Ireland and it became an amenity which attracted tourists in great numbers. It used electric power, but did not operate in strong winds. There were marvellous views of Bray and the surrounding area. Safety was paramount and during the years of its operation, from 1950 to 1970, there was never a serious incident.

The Cottage, Eagle's Nest Café, Bray, *c.*1953. At the upper end of the chair-lift on Bray Head was the Eagle's Nest restaurant and ballroom. Every Tuesday, visitors to the Red Island Holiday Camp were given a day out to Bray, including a ride on the chair-lift to the Eagle's Nest Café for lunch. The ballroom did well in the summer evenings. Top show bands were featured and, together with the Arcadia ballroom in Bray, it was a favourite venue for dancers.

Greystones, looking up Church Road from the railway station, *c.*1907. Jaunting cars and carriages wait outside the station.

Interior of the railway station at Greystones, *c.*1910. There is a train approaching the platform for the waiting passengers. In the distance, there is a footbridge over the line. It is interesting to note the weighing machine on the platform on the left. Even in 1910, people were conscious about their weight!

The Grand Hotel, Trafalgar Road, Greystones, *c*.1930. At the back of the hotel were grounds with tennis courts overlooking the beach. Hotel advertisements stated that the locality was three degrees on average warmer than Bournemouth and four inches less in rainfall.

A peaceful scene in Trafalgar Road, Greystones, around 1930, as a lady crosses the road pushing a pram. The shops on the right are Samuel Ferns, draper and Emily Greer, stationer and newsagent. The sender of the card is staying at the next building, which is the Central Hotel. There is a sign on its side to say the hotel is fully licensed and has a garage. In the distance, a flag flies over the Grand Hotel.

Church Road, Greystones, *c.*1910. Two gentlemen stroll in the middle of the road and pass the shop of Mr C.E. Doyle, a grocer and hardware merchant, at Stanley Place.

Church Road, Greystones, from the railway station *c.*1955. Compared with 1907 (see p. 123), the traffic on the road has increased. The buildings on the left look similar but there are a number of new shops on the right.

The Boating Slip, Greystones, *c.*1940. There are quite a lot of swimmers in the water. The boats were for hire for fishing. The postcard was published locally by McKenzie at no. 2 Trafalgar Road.

A further postcard published by McKenzie showing the South Beach at Greystones, *c.*1940. This was a very popular sandy beach with safe bathing. There was a charge for using the bathing huts and some people are choosing to get changed behind them.